Plague Poems

March, April, May
2020

33 poems written by three friends, one each per week on themes set during the height of the coronavirus pandemic

Introduction

It started with a frustrated desire to do something other than work. Two friends began setting a weekly theme for each other to write a poem about. Those two expanded to three, with a fourth cheering, considerately from the page margins and occasionally, self-deprecatingly offering some words of her own.

Then a pandemic spread around the world like frost across a window pane. We would all be having our lives simplified for some time. There were hours reclaimed in our days from struggling to and from work, travelling to meetings and visiting people. Our weekly writing challenge shifted subtly from something squeezed into spare minutes, to being more like the mind equivalent of the cherished, permitted daily stroll under lockdown. It became a thing to look forward to, a moment when we could switch outlooks, breathe, and more quietly take notice of what was happening around us.

We don't know if we are poets, but we are people who write poetry. And, there is a way in which the brain works differently when you give it permission to express itself in the language and forms of the poem. It seems to make sense of experience, assimilate and pattern the world differently to other ways of observing. That feels like a good thing.

Why would we want to bring these together to share them? Partly because making things is fun and, once done, allows you to move on and do something else. That's as true for carving a spoon as playing with words. Of course, the more you do it, hopefully there's that hope that you might get better at it too.

That is how we have ended up with 33 poems written over the three peak, initial months of the pandemic in the UK. All of us found some release, delight, distraction and opportunity to reflect in a different way on the strangeness of the changes in our lives. We make no great literary claims for our output. In style they range from pure whimsy, to haiku, free form and a sonnet. In subject matter they vary from immediate responses to the crisis, to shared cultural memories sparked by our messaging each other, yet experienced by each of us very differently. Some are obvious like ‘infection’ and ‘the skull of the virus’. Others were triggered by the conditions of the crisis, like the sound of birdsong revealed more clearly by the reduction in traffic and the fact that, suddenly, everyone appeared to be baking bread. ‘Cortina’ was suggested because to some it felt like we were back in the 1970s and the ubiquitous Ford car seemed synonymous with the decade. ‘Together’ was because we couldn’t be. The poems appear in the order in which they were written and shared amongst us. We keep that order here because it is entirely possible that it influenced what we wrote.

If all they are is just a different kind of brief diary, reflecting an unusual time, then that too is enough. The sections that follow are simply structured around the word set as the thematic challenge for each week. At the very least we hope our Plague Poems might hold a sense of how it has been, and perhaps entertain or intrigue you.

Andrew, Nicky & Nick

May 2020

1. Infection

Like soft blossoms from her hands
I saw an old woman
hang knitted decorations
in a tree, and wanted to do
something blessed too

Good habits, bad habits
the odd virus - to think
we could live without
picking things up

All spread through contact
that local way to say 'hello'
favoured gods, fashion too
as it's designed to do
   tunes like worms in the apple
of your ear, eat inwards
are passed on in hum

It's people of course
who most get under the skin
can infect your mood with a look
a slight, delayed response

But the morning can catch
me just as much, sun leaking
through feelings as if drawn curtains
early birdsong burning-off
night-curdled grudges

Contagion is the general rage
where tiny viral despots hide
bide their time, hitch rides
on you to conquer the next town
lethal and not, like life
itself super-spreads. Remember
   you caught that also

Andrew

When he crawled from the first fertile swamp
Pale gills flapping feebly
Lungs rasping as he sucked in sharp new air
Did the earth not shudder in premonition?

Did the shadow of future greed, war and filth
Not flicker across that ancient forest?
Did not the black rocks bark their warnings -
Unclean. Unclean.

Sodden bandages cling now to rotten stumps
Festering sores pupate the dead soil
Spores flay in the fetid scum

We are all unclean.

Nicky

I fashioned me a pomander
of rosemary and bay
and sprinkled in some budding mint
that I reckoned would me save
from the fogs and infections
that cloud our crowded isle.
And every time I took a draught
my selfish soul did smile.

I crafted one for my lady love.
She wore it night and day.
But these fragrant fumes failed us both
and the plague did get its way.

Only reason and solidarity
can deflect infection's curse.
So if you aim to see this through
let your neighbour be your nurse.

Nick

2. Birds

Here they come again
without a by your leave
millions of undocumented migrants
swarming and swooping
and singing across our borders
to be greeted with a joy
as boundless as the Norfolk sky.

Darling Swallow, speedy Swift
and Martins of sand and home
serenade us once more
with your African tunes
that pulse with springtime
and tell that summertime's soon.

Nick

Someone knew
what would happen to Icarus
if it was birds, a good bet
why did they say nothing?

Maybe they saw him ignore
his father. Thought, 'why bother?'
Birds have past on this: flying off
before disasters - earthquakes, hurricanes
without a word; dying-out when
preyed-on, no warning of the consequences
  Questions tickle like ruffled feathers
not a single answer tweeted

Back to Icarus, it wasn't the cat
curiosity killed, but him wanting to know
what 'bird-like' was
  bird-brain more like, without a crow's
problem solving skills, or bony magnetite
to compass a decent migration
  Not for feather boy
the parliament of owls
more a sleep with the fishes

Birds, they keep their counsel
inheritance-minded, don't share
with us secrets picked-up through
telephone wires and on the wing
never mention the maligned
dinosaur ancestors. They're happy
just to watch us humans fly
too high like Icarus
and wait

Andrew

Every day at the same time
An arrow of geese cross overhead
Honking from pond to pond
Like a group of old friends
Bantering from pub to pub
Improbably heavy, with slow wing beats
They firmly but gently suspend disbelief
I don't know why
But they bring me unspeakable joy
Rising in my chest as a bubble of laughter
Emerging uncontrollably as a human hoot
Head back, arms flung wide, a small star on a muddy field,
I shout back to the sky GEESE!

Nicky

3. A Loaf of Bread

I look through the window
as if it is an oven door
something outside is cooking

At least I hope so
my stomach murmurs
like an expectant crowd and
the cupboard is empty

Silent streets
bright as an empty room
blossom only keeping company
turn a corner, two
nobody still, buttered
toasted, daydreams fill
my head, I am in search
of a loaf of bread

Small paving stones look up
so many scattered slices
I look back to long gone
Saturdays, the fresh White Tin
whose crust tapped like a dull drum
brought from Woods the baker by
my overworked mother
iced finger buns too
I've not tasted since, or

that black bread from the Black Forest
it shocked me, heavy as the underworld
dark as the Tin loaf was light
a flavour of confusion like freedom
on a first foreign trip. How
could it be so different and
still be bread? By then, of course

we'd taken to this phoney stuff, sheets
of soft blown foam, denatured
fresh or stale did not apply
no asking why, we caught
the crumbs, I think, of what

they made for astronauts, and
just called it modern

Slow rising memories
stop outside the shop, 'Closed'
a note – 'We hope, but don't know
when we'll open next'.

Here's the line, no thicker
than a good crust
how many loaves from anarchy?
Order, all fine one side
danger and broken trust the other

If you've slept outside, unprotected
only imagined a bed, you'll know
what dough, still oven-warm does
to the hungry. Unfamiliar queues
unwanted clues that even big shops
like big brother, can't be relied on

I carry my empty bag like a sad stadium
the road, unpeopled, houses
looking down, disappointed fans
Then the aroma comes through
one of these windows
like a messenger pushing through
masses with good news
a welcome of ages
a stopper of riots
a rounded warmth we
can break and share

Like waking, it seems
too simple, knowing
we can bake our
own way out

Andrew

She'd kept it back for me
a little piece of virus luxury
its scabbed and dented
helmet-head,
onto which sweet walnuts
are softly spread.

I saw them blossom
in Californian heat.
I saw the plains
where grew the wheat.
I saw the grains
then ground to dust.
I saw it rise
and grow its crust.

It lies before me,
some words are spoken.
Bread is complete
when it is broken.

Nick

I held the loaf just as my grandma liked
Beneath her arm - and sliced across the end
The crust went crunch and then the creamy white
Gave to the knife as to a new made friend.
Two eggs await, a-bubble on the ring
A china plate in blue, with eastern scenes
The bread must toast become before the ping
A meal, a life, to share - all this bread means.
Two egg cups ready (useless but for this)
The toaster jumps and I dance there and back
My fingers smart - what sacrifice for bliss!
Slim soldiers now laid out upon the rack
Full dressed in marmite ready for the feast
I dip them in the egg brains like a beast.

Nicky

4. Melted

Parked inside the old school gates
where home-time skinheads
wave letters of hate
the ice cream van sells playtime treats

Lining-up like wasps, willing at a trap
we buzz, chaos and energy, determined
to have life, whatever the cost
to ourselves or, oblivious, others

Shouts and balls bounce of walls that
trick us with their permanence
we don't grasp at all we're
only passing through, that
nothing will be safe: the school field
local library, the buses, the bricks
the school itself. These houses
outside the gates, built for everyone
the idea that we were supposed
to be there for each other
not just queuing for ourselves

Wrapped in flags just like the haters
Tories came to power, promised hope and
harmony, planned discord and despair
a great unravelling, drawn out
like late summer shadows across the playground

We glimpsed it only in news, plots unfolding
that to win confused. Besides, it was break time
I'd saved 10 pence for a bigger ice cream
soft-whipped white trophy in my winner's hands

It was two victorious licks, then a football
kicked, took it. Not just that
fragile as the broken cone, tears
and laughs took my pride
the ice cream fell like a generation
hit hot tarmac, and did its thing

Andrew

My ice cube in your cocktail
Gave itself body and soul
To a greater cause.

Nicky

Shapeshifter planet,
you mess with my head
your bloodstream is lava,
cold winter is dead
tall candles dissolve
at your shrine by the sea
that each moment rises,
ever closer to me.

Your iceflows are fev'rish,
your mountains they sweat
your treasures are liquified
into lagoons of regret.

Shapeshifter planet,
we swim to your aid;
let goldfinches flicker
and show us the way.

Nick

5. Together

Singly, shly in creamy robes they come
Swaying with their first gulp of spring
Sash'd in polka-d green.

Huge armed, wild gestures branching
Skin long nobbled, herding the young
O what fine dances they once led!

Knee-high scampers burst into song
Circling edgeland ballrooms
Driving their parents nuts .

My loves, Birch, Oak and Hazel bright
I must leave you now
A Crow calls me south.

Nick

I never understood the maudlin creed
that we enter and leave this world alone
We couldn't be closer at the start
by the time we're done, we've
scattered ourselves in heads and hearts
Not much could make us more together
like sown crops we wait upon the weather

Seeds of barley, oats or wheat, we need
talk and touch, like sun and rain to grow
More than metaphor we have these things
that make us live through others: mirror neurons,
lying still when we're alone, on contact they fling
us into cabarets of copied feeling
we're all puppet-masters, everyone is reeling

Self made man is myth. Who taught you
how to tie your shoes, cleaned your milky chin
Who unlocked books, cooked and passed the ball
Who knows your name, keeps your secrets
Ignores all faults and takes your call
however hard the days, remember from that start
there never was just you, there never was apart.

Andrew

My heart was a colt made to race,
Bucking in a bright green field,
Growing strong, flexible muscle,
Pumping iron, breathing fire.

You arrived in a cool breeze
Unsettling and yet a comfort
In a casual cloak of storm
And as flames in a forest, we cleared the fence
Branded alike against that thunderous sky
Close forged like the many layered steel of Japanese dreams.

Nicky

6. Switch

They say it helps to turn it off and on again
But that assumes you can find a switch
What if the world is gone beyond control
Or off is one-way only, deep down in a ditch?

Currents carry crowds with momentum as consent
Few try against the tide, dam or divert the flow alone
Yet switch we do as salmon swim upstream, the driver
Takes a bike instead, a frequent flier stays at home

Chameleon, we are a mess of sparky wet electrics
More kind than self-preserving in a crisis
When nature or a system-break hits reset and
No one is the puppet of some dead economist

Off went the commute to work, the crowded shopping trip
On came quiet streets, the online conference call
Switches flicking all around like a clapping circuit board
Treasures found by lifting stones, and people walking tall.

Andrew

Once bowed
by winter's cold compress
Now bathed
in April's sweet liqueur
I saw you rise,
rise from last year's mud & mould
I saw you unfurl,
unfurl & stretch
towards the empty sky.

Ballerina of the forest floor,
miracle of the fronded fern
how much higher
can you now go?

Nick

A slender slip, a young shoot
That could have been a mighty tree
Swishing through the bendy air
To bash grass heads on the verge.
Silky seed heads in clumpy tufts
And smooth rocket shapes explode skyward
Wanton destruction flinging life about
Like the dandelion herself.
No - today, in the dappled light, in this lane
I wouldn't swap places with anyone.

Nicky

7. The Lie of the Land

Never worked, or so you'd think, barren
uplands, empty as mountains on Mars
The odd, hovering camera only reminding of us

It isn't true of course, wasn't always that way
Every tree was eagerly felled before some
painter, conned, came to honour
desecration for a gallery wall

People too were removed, or pictured
like idling sheep, grazing happily in place
not displaced like the trees. But gone they were
to cities buzzing like hives, overworked
where other lies are told, such as
'there is no space for nature'

Then Blackbird sings, 'That's not so'
Nightfox glances, 'Watch me go'
Branches of a Gingko tree that brushed
the skin of dinosaurs, has leaves that breathe
our toxic air and, you know, it does not care

Bees prefer our gardens, parks
the diet is better, dogs bark
at squirrels who vanish up twisted trunks
laugh down from above
don't mess with me, punk

It keeps you guessing – nature – jokes with life
puts little where you expect, where not it's rife
hides the lies for us to look, listen, discover
how we might step back to let the land recover

Andrew

Six thousand springtimes separate us,
six thousand summers too.
This whale-backed chamber
planted here to hold the lie of the land:
the pyramid of chalk and turf,
he slinking stream and imperial road,
the soft ascent and doorway cold

How many years will I erase In my next step?
Yet before I can enter in
a Swallow corkscrews out of the dark,
screaming life, crying liberty
heading south across the grasslands
south towards the salted sea.

Nick

That familiar shape, a thigh-curved swelling of the land
Swooping down past buzzing mustard fields of yellow
Edged with soft green pasture lace.
Clumps of woodland, scruffy and secret
Known only to the foot of fox, badger, stoat.
Ridden first in a jolting pushchair
Every flint a brake on the stuttering wheels,
Then by bike, fleet and fearless as a young swift,
Avoiding the gravel patch where Keith came a cropper,
With Dad, Cortina straining to reach a ton.
I can shut my eyes and feel the camber still;
The lie of the land lies within me.

Nicky

8. Cortina

We hunted adders in the forest
Behind every tumulus a Saxon
Behind every cumulus a Spitfire
Yes, I liked the Supermarine's speed
but it could only fly.
Now the Catalina could fly and swim,
forever landing in far-away waters
of placid warmth.

Red-handed from blackberry picking
Me and Mark rushed to his Dad's car
It was then I noticed its name
"Mr Jones, it's great you're driving a Catalina,
like the flying boats that were in the war..."
"Son, it's a Cortina named after some Italian girl..."

In the laughter, I learned what farce is
Soon after I got my first pair of glasses.

Nick

Born in Essex, it was like driving a Ford Cortina
people made judgements: flash, fast-looking
but cheap, a bit above yourself
You might strike a pose, but nobody rose
a future parked within yards of your front door

We fell for it too, looked up to the first families
whose cars had electric windows, joked
about Daddy picking us up in a Roller

I was a child of the great car economy
So great they cut thirteen concrete lanes
through my home town, carved the community
with a Berlin Wall of traffic. You'll say no one
got shot, but my friend Ian, he flew as high
as a fence, hit on his walk to school
And everyone had inhalers, struggled for breath
as we tried to work out the world

Teachers made options easier, took us
to the factory making Cortinas, 'picture
yourself on a production line, do enough time
you might buy one'. Have a go
keep the show on the roads that creep
like varicose veins across your countryside

No alternative they said, even as
the protests spread. We were in the back seats
of our own lives, being driven dangerously
'Maggie and Ron' written in swirly on the bonnet

Ever since I've looked for the handle
Tried to disable the child lock
Wanted out, to draw the curtain
wanted to shout about the cliff edge
coming at us like a drunken
boy racer in a red Cortina GT

Now we know what it takes to hit
the brakes, how one pandemic pauses
another, and what it's like to live
without a flooding river of cars, with
air that's clear enough to peer
along the road ahead and wonder
Now, can we take a different one instead

Andrew

It was my mums idea
To save space in the boot
What with four kids in the back
Snuggling, bickering, eye spy and bottom jokes
Let's use Tesco bags instead of suitcases.

Oh how we mocked them
With their British flapping plastic
Ineptly strapped on roof racks
As we glided past, sleek Cortina shark.

We catnapped in lay-bys
Mum shushing, dad trying to sleep
Us dozing in a puppy heap
Til we tumbled out in French France, sun blazing
Fresh fish on blocks of ice
Squats with feet shapes
Thinly sliced garlic sausage and red, red wine.

The bags didn't really work as they all looked the same
I wore your pants and you mine
Once ironed shirts crumpled to smithereens
Salty, sandy, rumpled shorts and skirts
Danced in the original jumble sale, pick and mix car boot.

Nicky

9. The Skull of the Virus

Inside its tiny, tiny virus head
like a shameful, buried family secret
reasons for the many, many dead
are dashed on scraps in private code

A zombie dedication to its killing task
airborne, drifting like old barbed sea mines
it crosses porous borders, does not ask
and said, on trial: 'I only followed genetic orders'

Under a black lapel, a bat skull pin
badge of the brotherhood, unlovers of life
Hell's Angels of handshakes, slander of pangolin
we open Pandora's box to put you back in

Andrew

A tardis bone chamber of fear
Tiny fragile vole skull head on
But glimpsed from the eye"s corner
In the small cold hours of the night
The looming terror of Tyrannosaurus Rex

Nicky

You wear a fine crown
but don't have a head.
Your spectral armies
are out harvesting our dead

What are your war aims
my invisible foe?
Why do you cling to us
like some viral FOMO?

Let's negotiate as equals,
a deal we will make.
We'll give you gold coin aplenty
now what will it take?

I see you don't answer
Is there more that you need?
Our nation is ravaged,
Our people do bleed.

Pandora is beckoning
This talking must stop
We must find our own path
to reseal the box

Blind Justice will lead us
with Reason forearmed
guided by Compassion
so that no-one is harmed

Your crown it is slipping
your host slinks away
We'll keep watch eternal
so the future is saved.

Nick

10. Hive

We found ourselves.
We found ourselves covered in a red dust
bitter, metallic, choking breath, clogging veins
and when it rained
the earth spat blood.

So we decided to build ourselves.
We decided to build ourselves a new hive
with a new language
a structure for social embracing
where the old and single Queen
was dethroned
where all were Queens
where all the walls were windows
where we saw the law
of immediate attraction
unfold in blossom unbounded.

And we ate ourselves.
We ate ourselves silly
giggling at the trickling stickiness
that sweet and honied flood
that sweet reward that had us licked.

Nick

Conversation waggle dances
well worn steps with
subtle shifts that tell me
where our friendship is

I fly to its flower, brush
against bright words
hoping for honey

We digress, drift
as if in a stiff breeze of
memory and news of others

Your face on screen
moving in its cell
recalls watching live bees
behind museum glass

We have fast become
more hive mind
for whom touch
is in the past

Andrew

Embraced in a bramble girdle
The hive waits
A grey weathered box
Until crowned again with the teeming sweetness of life

Nicky

11. Peak

At the peak, dust and crag
everything is below
or behind me
no 'there' there
bare of living, but
for views back and down

It brought me here though
dragged mutinous donkey legs
from bed to breakfast
out the door, a rucksack
to gather what happens
swapping cables overhead
for clouds; hot, flat asphalt
for rooty, rising trails

   where you have to pay attention
stop for the rocks, the drop
sunbathing snakes, orchids
in cracks. Before the top
over your shoulder
a horizon rises, looms
in surprise like Earth
from the moon

All you have to do
is walk, wonder is free
for that I'll climb again

Andrew

So, what caused it then?

A pall of volcanic dust
from far-away Cathay
blotting out the rays
of our beloved summer sun?

Or, some ecstatic shudder
in the self-same sun's
quite muddled race
through the singing
spheres of space?

Or, ourselves perhaps
that plague we gave
(with enslavement attached)
to the welcoming peoples
whose kingdoms now
lie beneath a spreading green?

No matter.

The path from Olympus' peak
was steep, sheer scree
I lost my father, mother
two small children too.

At its feet,
heads cracked, bodies bruised
we crawled, scrabbled
and then stood.

From the south,
a Crow flew fast,
circled once and landed,
waddled a few steps
and croaked
this strange request:

"In silence please,
answer three questions
and so guide your feet
across the plain
to those distant peaks:

What will you keep,
What you leave behind
And will you do anew?"

First scared
then puzzled
and finally
a friendly frown,
a sly smile
on the faces
of my friends
and beloved ones

Inside my rattled skull,
I made my choice

To keep, two tales
a sermon from another peak
and an epic from an Asian beach,
that squabble over a wooden horse.

To leave behind:
all notions of dominion,
one over another,
ourselves over
our broken mother Nature
and our self
over our precious self.

And to do anew?
I'll keep that to myself
thank you.

And so
each carrying a triple treasury
cherished,
unburdened,
inspired
to wild discovery,
our ragged crew set off
following the Crow's looping flight
to the distant snow-caps
now gilded in returning light.

Nick

Is this it?
The icy pinnacle we sought for so many years
Grappling with equipment, straps, clips and ties
Dragging it all up here into the clean air
Our nylon flapping and snapping in the wind

Is this it?
The deep leather chair stolen from so many calves
Rotating sumptuously between glass screens
Silent and controlled; just a bit too cold
Keening the cityscape as eagles pass effortlessly

Is this it?
The polished podium of power, a sea of upturned faces
Lifted in anticipation of words of wisdom
What could we possibly say that would add a jot
To our need for warmth and love and hearts joining.

Nicky

Any profits from the sale of this volume are being donated to the London-based community organisation Living Under One Sun www.livingundersun.co.uk.

Acknowledgements:

We want to thank David Boyle of the Real Press and John Jackson of The Argument by Design.

Anita Roy was hugely enthusiastic and encouraging with this project and also was moved to join in twice with these contributions:

The World Upside Down

Outside is emptied in.
Houses stoppered, brimming,
Stuffed with family.

The sky unscored,
Air minus planes,
Virgin Mary blue.

Birds, unfurtive,
Strut about like they own the place.

Icefloes uncalve
Heave themselves from the water
Like walrus
And silently knit
Back together crystal
By crystal.

The Lie of the Land

The land does not lie
But its people.

Biographies:

Nick, Nicky and Andrew are also among the contributors to three collections of modern folk tales for troubling times also published by The Real Press: *There was a Knock at the Door*, *Knock Twice*, and *Knock Three Times*.

Nick Robins is a historian diverted into the world of finance and sustainability by the climate crisis. Since 2018, he has been Professor in Practice for Sustainable Finance at the London School of Economics. He previously co-directed UNEP's Inquiry into a Sustainable Financial System and established HSBC's Climate Change Centre. He has helped to set up Carbon Tracker and Planet Tracker. He has published widely on sustainability issues (including *Sustainable Investing: the Art of Long-term Performance*). But his real passion is rethinking the past and in 2006 published *The Corporation that Changed the World: How the East India Company Shaped the Modern Multinational*; he is currently exploring the climate history of southern England. Twitter: @nvjrobins1

Nicky Saunter is an Economist-trained editor who became a serial collaborator and starter of things with other people, including the Boston Tea Party coffee house group, The Woolly Shepherd acoustics firm, natural training social enterprise Learning from the Land and most recently the wildlife and landscape restoration charity, Beaver Trust. In between, she writes poems and stories, and prints monochrome photographs, heavily influenced by her rural life. If she could change into an animal, she would.

Andrew Simms is a political economist, environmentalist and co-founder of the New Weather Institute, coordinator of the Rapid Transition Alliance and assistant director of Scientists for Global Responsibility. He is a research associate at the Centre for Global Political Economy, University of

Sussex, and a fellow of the New Economics Foundation (nef), where he was policy director for many years. His books include *Tescopoly* and *Ecological Debt.* He co-authored *The New Economics, Eminent Corporations,* and the original *Green New Deal*, devising the concept of 'Earth Overshoot Day' to illustrate when we begin living beyond our environmental means. He recently wrote a beginner's guide to economics from a heterodox perspective, *Economics: A Crash Course,* with David Boyle, the first of its kind, and his book, *Cancel the Apocalypse: the New Path to Prosperity* is a manifesto of new economic possibilities. Twitter: @andrewsimms_uk